Watch Her Bloom
Mark Anthony

bagabond
75455 Wilshire Boulevard,
Los Angeles, CA 90036

Mark Anthony is a bestselling poet from Seattle whose previous works include, "Soulmates," "Soulmates II," "Heart and Soul," and "Inspiration."

He is happily married to his one true love, and continues to live the life he's always wanted by being bold, and following his heart.

You can follow him

on Instagram @markanthonypoet

And Facebook @markanthonypoet

For my beautiful daughter,
who lives the truth of these
words on the daily.

WATCH HER BLOOM

poetic affirmations to help you
heal, grow, and move on.

Sometimes words can heal us
better than any medicine.

She's changed.

You can see it in her face,
and in her walk,
and in the way
she knows where
she's going
and doesn't look back.

Mark Anthony

And then one day
she just decided
she would live for herself,
and not for others,
and nobody
had the power
to make her
unhappy
ever again

You deserve the love you give,
the smiles you bring,
the happiness you share.

You deserve the kisses you leave,
the embraces you gift,
and the life you've always wanted.

She refused to compete
with anyone but herself,
and you could always tell
she was winning
by the size of the smile
on her face.

WATCH HER BLOOM

If you have flaws,
don't hide them
for those
who truly love you
will see beauty in them
simply because
they are part of you.

Mark Anthony

Never doubt
the road you're on
is the one
you're supposed to be on.

Everyone's path
leads to their higher purpose
in the end.

Heartbreak lasts
as long as you need to grieve
and learn how to treat yourself
as well as they should have
when you were together.

Even when she was lonely
there were nights
when she forgot to be sad,
and she would find herself
singing along
to some old song on the radio,
and it was like the entire world
was now her companion,
as slowly and surely
she remembered how to feel love
in all the hidden places inside of her
where she had forgotten to look.

Never give up on your dreams
for they are your birthright,
and you owe it to yourself
to become the beautiful badass you are.

There's somebody out there for you,
somebody who will get your soul
and tend to your heart like a flower,
but you must be patient as the rain,
as the sea, as the sky,
because finding love is part of nature,
and it will not bloom until its season.

What you wanted from love was right,
but it was with the wrong person.

Believe me, somebody will fall in love
with you 're kind of crazy.

The mistakes we make in love
are only the lessons we need
to discover a love that lasts.

We have to know what breaks us,
before we can stay unbroken.

Mark Anthony

She had to walk away,
not because she didn't love him,
but because she had to love herself more.

Hurt feelings, if not grieved,
stay frozen inside of us
long after the loss,
until we become numb,
and end up making
the same mistakes over and over,
but after we face the hurt, grieve,
and let it go, we find the tears
have helped us float down the river
to where we truly belong.

Forgive yourself
for everything.

You are only learning
what it means to be human.

Mark Anthony

Take a little time each day
to appreciate the simple things in life,
especially in your relationships,
and you will have already discovered
one of the great secrets of lasting love.

Mark Anthony

WATCH HER BLOOM

You're fully at peace with yourself,
comfortable and beautiful in your own skin,
so please remain patient,
wait for somebody who sees your light
and honors the work you've done.

Beware of the ones who don't know themselves,
the ones who can't feel,
and need you to do all the emotional work for them.

Mark Anthony

The universe is not trying to break you,
it's trying to find a way to wake you up,
so that you will see what's real and worth
fighting for.

It takes time to heal but it also takes love
and courage.

And so one day
she discovered
she was fierce,
and strong,
and full of fire,
and that not even she
could hold herself back
because her passions
burned brighter than her fears.

Mark Anthony

Don't let anyone make you
think you're crazy,
just because they're frightened
that you have the courage to feel.

Mark Anthony

She doesn't settle for less
than her soul deserves,
and when she sets her sights
on something,
she doesn't stop dreaming,
until it's come true.

And so she learned
that love was something
you couldn't force.

You had to trust the universe
would bring your soul
exactly what it needed
to complete itself,
and only you were ready
to receive its gifts.

Relationships are never perfect,
so we have to keep learning
how to listen with our hearts,
and see each other's souls
as clearly as our own.

We have to be careful of ego, pride
and overthinking.

If we can no longer listen
or be touched by somebody's words,
it doesn't matter what we say,
because nobody feels loved.

Emotions aren't something to be feared,
but a sign that you're alive,
and trying to find your truth.

Know that numbness is a far far
more dangerous thing.

You're important,
you're deserving,
you're worth it,
you're beautiful,
you're strong,
you're perfect as you,
you're rare,
you're real,
you're you.

Mark Anthony

You deserve a love
who tells you they care,
a love who listens
when you speak,
a love who chooses you
above the rest,
because they know
you have the missing
piece of their soul.

It's time to start taking yourself
out on dates,
doing what you love to do,
so you remember how O K you were
before you met them,
and that you're still the same charming
soul
you've always been,
as you make a toast to yourself
and smile.

Every path to healing a broken heart
begins with the desire
to turn the chaos of your life
into a work of art,
so find a way to paint yourself whole
again,
until you can see yourself in the big picture,
and the beauty of how it all worked out
for the best.

You've always been
more than enough,
you just need to find the one
who could see it.

If you begin a relationship
based on seduction
instead of sincerity,
whatever is left unspoken
when you were playing games
will be the very thing that breaks you up
in the end.

Act boldly,
from a place of sincere love,
and great forces will always come
to your assistance.

Mark Anthony

WATCH HER BLOOM

If you haven't found
the love of your life yet,
it doesn't mean they're not out there,
it just means the time isn't right,
and timing in love is everything.

Mark Anthony

If they don't deserve you,
part of them knows it,
so they will sabotage themselves,
and the relationship
because they lack the courage
to admit it,
so take their departure
as a blessing in disguise,
and move on to find
the one who knows
they deserve somebody
as beautiful and unique as you.

Mark Anthony

You are worth more
than you give yourself credit for,
just think back on all the bad-ass things
you've done,
and remember that was you who did them,
and it is you who will do them again.

The love of your life
is searching for you,
without knowing your name,
but already knowing,
the secret yearning of your heart.

Broken-hearted girls
become women warriors
who change the world.

Mark Anthony

If you're on the right path in life,
you will know it
by the effortlessness of your steps,
the beauty of your surroundings,
and the lack of hurry you feel
to get to the end.

She finally found the courage
to say goodbye to maybe's.

Some relationships teach us
what we don't want,
and some relationships teach us
we can have it all.

Feelings in a relationship
come and go like clouds,
so be patient,
and wait for the calm
after the storm,
then speak from your heart,
and not from your fear.

I hope that one day
you find the love you deserve.

I hope that one day
you find a love
that inspires your best self.

I hope that one day
you find the love
that gives you peace,
and makes you believe
that dreams come true.

One day you will discover
that your pain
was just pointing
to the places
where you needed
to heal most.

Don't be fooled
by the word love,
as it means
many different things
to many different people,
but your task is always
to find out what it means to them.

It's so easy to forget
that sometimes love
is just listening without judgment
or agenda,
listening with an open heart
and mind,
a humble willingness to see
your story in mine.

Your life is your life,
so don't let anybody tell you
that you can't make
your dreams come true
or live happily ever after.

Your life is your life,
so follow your heart
to where it wants to be,
and start living the life
you know one day
you will look back on
with a deep,
and knowing smile.

Choose the one
who chooses you,
and can tell you
all the reasons why.

Thank you for being you,
for being open,
for being alive,
for being curious,
for being funny,
for being worried about the world,
for being beautiful,
for being brave,
for being wild.

Thank you for being you.

Mark Anthony

First, understand your worth.

Second, don't ever settle for less

Eventually, you will forget
the lonely nights,
the questions,
and all the days
that seemed to fold into paper ships,
and sailed into the horizon.

Eventually, you will find a love so strong,
it will erase the mistakes of the past,
and bring you into a more constant present
where every day will be filled with more
light,
and laughter,
and yesterday will seem like a dream
you woke up from,
and never fell back asleep.

Happiness
is not acquired with more things,
but by opening one's eyes
in gratitude
for the things one already has.

Mark Anthony

Healing from heartbreak
takes more than time,
and tears,
and days when
you feel alone.

It takes picking yourself up
to face the day,
and trusting somehow
the darkness won't last forever,
and that the sun is just waiting for you
to find yourself again,
and to remember the light
that nobody can take away
from you.

It is important
to celebrate the little things,
to take time to tell somebody
you like their haircut
or appreciate their smile.

Life is too short not to notice,
even the smallest poems
that make up a beautiful book.

Mark Anthony

There was a time
when she waited for love,
when all she had was herself,
and her questions and doubts,
but she loved herself enough
to know she would wait
as long as she needed
to find somebody
who would love her,
the way she deserved,
the way she already loved herself.

I will never take for granted
what the universe has given me
in love and life,
in miracles, friends and family.

I feel gratitude for every moment
I get to share, every smile,
every breath that leads me
back to the ones I love.

Don't let anybody tell you
you're small or insignificant
because you are life itself,
searching for sunlight.

You are a flower, a bird,
the ocean, an earthquake,
a storm,
a poem being recited
by the Earth.

It trembles when you tremble,
breathes when you breathe,
and loves when you love,
so what are you waiting for?

This moment is all you have,
and this moment
is more than enough time
to break the universe into song.

Mark Anthony

Let go of everything
that hangs heavy
on your soul,
and you will find
the light
that sets
you free.

WATCH HER BLOOM

Open your heart to love,
but don't let anybody in
who isn't willing to protect it.

Mark Anthony

You deserve a love for all times,
especially hard times.

Mark Anthony

Don't lose sleep over somebody
who isn't dreaming of you.

WATCH HER BLOOM

She's tired of being taken advantage of.
She's tired of holding on to nothing.
She's tired of not being a priority.
She's tired of lies and empty promises.

So be the one she can rest her head on.
Be the one who lets her sleep.

Mark Anthony

If he's not making the effort,
he's not worth your time

Mark Anthony

She wanted more.
She felt trapped.
She felt hurt,
but she kept
fighting for herself,
until she became courageous
and strong
and capable of moving on.

She became the hero of her own story,
and the muse of her own art of living.

She survived the worst
in order to become her best

Physical attraction
is only part of the formula.
You also need laughter,
music, good food and friendship.

You need honesty,
trust, humility,
and a willingness
to walk through the fire.

To have a broken heart
is to know you're capable of love,
and if you're capable of loving once,
I promise you
you're capable of loving again,
only more deeply and wisely than before.

Mark Anthony

She found the courage to move on,
and heart ready for real love.

WATCH HER BLOOM

You won't forgive yourself for your mistakes,
until you start to see them
as the lessons you needed
to grow into somebody strong enough
to love and be loved through all seasons.

Mark Anthony

You deserve to be loved,
and appreciated for who you are,
not who they think you should be.

Never stop being the real you.

You are brave and beautiful.

Be kind to yourself.

Take each day as it comes,
and don't worry too much
about the future.

It's never too late to begin again,
and create the life you've always wanted.

Mark Anthony

One day all the heartbreak in your life
will be nothing more than
a distant memory,
and the love of your life will be the love
of your life.

Heartbreak teaches us
to take care of fragile things

Mark Anthony

Relationships that last are sometimes
as difficult as ones that don't,
so it becomes a question of whether or not
this is the one with whom you want
to share the work of love.

She's done chasing
better versions of herself,
and acting as she isn't perfect as she is.
She's tired of taking herself back to the
store,
as if she's broken, flawed
or not what she wanted.

From now on she's going to take herself
out in whatever condition she's in,
and rise like a kite high
above the rooftops.

From now on she's going to say,
"I love being this crazy damn kite,
and there will never be another one like it
again."

Nobody escapes childhood
without some scars to remind them
of where they've been
and where they need to heal,
but if you know this,
you can learn to be patient with yourself,
and others,
as everyone is fighting some hidden battle,
and trying to recover
the beauty of innocent things.

Remember love
is calm,
and infinite as the sea,
and never needs
to be rushed.

If it's mean to be,
it's meant to be.

Love is not what breaks you,
it's what heals you.

It's mistaking love
for something else that hurts.

I hope that all these words I write you
remind you that you are loved,
admired and adored,
and will one day be
tattooed upon your soul
so deeply,
you will never have
to read these words again
because you will know
all of them by heart,
and they will simply be part of you.

WATCH HER BLOOM

A
Afghanistan
Albania
Algeria
Andorra
Angola
Antigua and Barbuda
Argentina
Armenia
Australia
Austria
Azerbaijan
B
Bahamas
Bahrain
Bangladesh
Barbados
Belarus
Belgium
Belize
Benin
Bhutan
Bolivia
Bosnia and Herzegovina
Botswana
Brazil
Brunei
Bulgaria
Burkina Faso
Burundi
C
Cabo Verde
Cambodia
Cameroon
Canada
Chad
Chile
China

Colombia
Comoros
Congo
Cote d'Ivoire
Croatia
Cuba
Cyprus
Czechia
D
Denmark
Djibouti
Dominica
E
Ecuador
Egypt
El Salvador
Eritrea
Estonia
Eswatini
Ethiopia
F
Fiji
Finland
France
G
Gabon
Gambia
Georgia
Germany
Ghana
Greece
Grenada
Guatemala
Guinea
Guinea-Bissau
Guyana
H
Haiti
Honduras
Hungary

I
Iceland
India
Indonesia
Iran
Iraq
Ireland
Israel
Italy
J
Jamaica
Japan
Jordan
K
Kazakhstan
Kenya
Kiribati
Kosovo
Kuwait
Kyrgyzstan
L
Laos
Latvia
Lebanon
Lesotho
Liberia
Libya
Liechtenstein
Lithuania
Luxembourg
M
Madagascar
Malawi
Malaysia
Maldives
Mali
Malta

Mauritania
Mauritius
Mexico
Micronesia
Moldova
Monaco
Mongolia
Montenegro
Morocco
Mozambique
Myanmar
N
Namibia
Nauru
Nepal
Netherlands
New Zealand
Nicaragua
Niger
Nigeria
North Korea
Norway
O
Oman
P
Pakistan
Palau
Palestine
Panama
Paraguay
Peru
Philippines
Poland
Portugal

THIS BOOK IS SOLD THROUGH RETAILERS IN THE FOLLOWING COUNTRIES AND MEETS ALL REGIONAL STATE, AND COUNTRY REQUIREMENTS AND REGULATIONS FOR EACH PRINTED IN THE UNITED STATES OF AMERICA.

84

Mark Anthony

Q
Qatar
R
Romania
Russia
Rwanda
S
Saint Kitts
and
Nevis
Saint Lucia
Saint Vincent and
the Grenadines
Samoa
San Marino
Sao Tome and
Principe
Saudi Arabia
Senegal
Serbia
Seychelles
Sierra Leone
Singapore
Slovakia
Slovenia
Solomon Islands
Somalia
South Africa
South Korea
South Sudan
Spain
Sri Lanka
Sudan
Suriname
Sweden
Switzerland
Syria

T
Taiwan
Tajikistan
Tanzania
Thailand
Timor-Leste
Togo
Tonga
Trinidad and
Tobago
Tunisia
Turkey
Turkmenistan
Tuvalu
U
Uganda
Ukraine
United Arab Emirates (U A E)
United Kingdom (U K)
United States of America (U S A)
Uruguay
Uzbekistan
V
Vanuatu
Vatican City (Holy See)
Venezuela
Vietnam
Y
Yemen
Z
Zambia
Zimbabwe

Published
BY 𝔟𝔞𝔤𝔞𝔟𝔬𝔫𝔡
www.vagabond.ltd
All rights reserved. No part of this book may be reproduced in any form on by an electronic or mechanical means, including information storage and retrieval systems, without permission in writing from the publisher, except by a reviewer who may quote brief passages in a review.

*001
EDITION

© 2021 MARK ANTHONY
POETthrough
SAINT AT
SEVENTH
www.vagabond.ltd

Your satisfaction of quality, delivery, and content of our products are very important to us: feedback.
saintmemory.com.

PRODUCT ID:
9237472832

www.ingramcontent.com/pod-product-compliance
Lightning Source LLC
Chambersburg PA
CBHW031457040426
42444CB00007B/1128